CULTURAL AMNESIA

THREE ESSAYS ON TWO KINGDOMS
THEOLOGY

BRIAN G. MATTSON

SWINGING BRIDGE PRESS

For Jeffery J. Ventrella,

They tell me that culture transformers do not exist.
I know better because I know you.

CONTENTS

FOREWORD BY JOSEPH BOOT

Early in his Sermon on the Mount, Jesus told his followers, "You are the light of the world. A city set on a hill
cannot be hidden. Nor do people light a lamp and put it
under a basket, but on a stand, and it gives light to all in
the house. In the same way, let your light shine before
others, so that they may see your good works and give
glory to your Father who is in heaven" (Matt. 5:14-16).

What is the source of that light? And what is the
nature of these good works? The light is *Christ himself*
who, by His Spirit, through the gospel of the kingdom,
drives away the darkness and translates us from the
kingdom and dominion of darkness into the kingdom of
light. These are the only *two kingdoms* that Scripture
recognizes, and they represent antithetical spiritual
conditions basic to the life of all people. Biblically, no
other ultimate dividing line runs through the integral
unity of God's cosmic creation (our temporal order)—
creation and redemption stand in an unbreakable historical continuum. The light exposes the spiritual antithesis

at work in the world and we are promised that darkness cannot overcome its illuminating presence. The works we are called to do are also the works of light, which are kingdom works grounded in truth and righteousness, or justice. Nothing in Scripture limits these works of light to ecclesiastical activities; indeed, these works are the totality of our life, because "we are his workmanship." The unity of God's world, God's work and God's revelation is everywhere seen in Scripture.

Nonetheless, artificial dualisms, which crept in early in the life of the church as the thought-forms of Greco-Roman culture were synthesized with scriptural teaching, have been regularly seen in church history. Today, variations of dialectical Two Kingdoms teaching are ubiquitous in evangelicalism, whether of an Anabaptist, Lutheran, Scholastic or "Reformed" flavor. Some radically divide the historical development of the Christian church and broader non-Christian culture, placing them on parallel tracks so that they do not meet, to the point where Christian involvement in civil government, the police or military is rejected. Others assert a radical discontinuity between creation and re-creation, the present age and the future age, postponing or shunting off the dynamic reality of the kingdom of God into eternity. Others posit a deep dichotomy between law and gospel, older and newer testaments, and old and new covenant, so that God's law is seen as having no relevance for culture. And still others create, by fiat, two distinct realms within reality, one common and the other redemptive, governed by different laws and norms, where most of life (familial, vocational, public and civic life) is lived within a non-redemptive realm that is destined for total destruction. There are numerous blends of these positions and themes, many Christians taking a pick-and-mix approach to a Two Kingdoms Christianity. It is little wonder the church in the West is in the midst of perhaps its most notorious historical flight from responsibility within culture. In short, much of the church, with great theological ingenuity, seems to be seeking to pull off a great escape from God's world, surrendering it to Satan.

In this short but penetrating book, Brian Mattson decisively demolishes the myth that the light of Christ, the light of Him who is creator, redeemer and reigning king, can be imprisoned within one narrow domain of creation or limited in its reach and jurisdiction. Mattson forces the reader to ask, is the light of Christ a local light, a regional light, a limited light, a sectarian light, or is Christ the light of the world—the one who gives light to every man? In other words, should not the healing light of Christ, through his people, flood every world-and-life-sphere from the family home to the church house, school house and court house? Which part of life, which recess within creation, is meant to remain in the shadows?

Granted, for most genuine Christians, *that* the light should shine is rarely questioned, but *where* it should be allowed to shine remains a matter of sharp dispute. Does the light shine only privately in the heart to draw men and women to faith in Christ so that they can be forgiven of sin, join the church and go to heaven, or does the light of the world also illuminate and heal our families, schools, work, businesses, governments and other social organizations? Mattson forces us to ask where Scripture leads us to believe that some parts of creation should not be illuminated by the transforming light of the gospel—including our cultural and social institutions.

I believe that the recent iteration of this doctrine that has come to be known as Reformed Two Kingdoms theology has its philosophical roots in the old scholastic (nature-grace) dualism advanced by Roman Catholicism. Its advocates set up artificial and unbiblical barriers to the reach of the light of Christ, and seek to restrict the kingdom of God inside the institutional church. In this short collection of essays, Mattson has provided an incisive, succinct, informative, and compelling refutation of this doctrine. He demonstrates that logically, exegetically, and by empirical observation, the Two Kingdoms understanding of Christianity's relationship to culture is irretrievably flawed, showing it to be a misrepresentation of the covenant promises of God, and an *a priori* capitulation to Gnostic and scholastic dualism. To speak, as Two Kingdoms advocates do, of a 'common' and a 'redemptive' kingdom, is to artificially divide created reality, faithlessly limit the sphere and scope of redemption, and presumptuously delimit the jurisdiction of Christ and His Word.

As important as it is to refute such a serious error—and Mattson has done this admirably—the real test of a mature, robust theological vision is not in its ability to critique other doctrines, but its living, active, Spirit-filled power to transform the world. On this front, he cites the examples of such Christian cultural champions as William Wilberforce and Herman Bavinck, whose efforts to bring Christian truth to bear on the alleged "common kingdom" of slave trading, academia, civil government, and the public square, effected real, lasting and godly change.

For these reasons I have returned time and again to Mattson's excellent critique and employed many of his arguments fruitfully in the work of cultural apologetics. He has offered one of the most powerful refutations of this doctrine to date and no pastor should be without this superb resource.

—Rev. Dr. Joseph Boot (M.A, Ph.D).

Founder, Ezra Institute for Contemporary Christianity and Westminster Chapel in Toronto, Canada.

PREFACE

Years ago I was privileged to deliver two of the following essays in lecture form for the annual conference of the *Center for Cultural Leadership*, whom I serve as Senior Scholar of Public Theology. At that time I was very much personally and professionally engaged in the theological issues surrounding Two Kingdoms Theology, particularly the version emanating from Westminster Seminary in California.

My interests have since taken me far afield from intramural theological and ecclesiastical debates. However, over the years these essays in various stages of completion have circulated privately among friends and acquaintances, and I am often asked to publish them for the edification of a wider audience. I have finally acquiesced to their request.

I will say that the intervening years have only strengthened my belief that Two Kingdoms Theology is untenable. In both its 16th century and present-day manifestations it is only conceivable in a culture already shaped by the very same Christian gospel its advocates claim does not shape culture or common institutions. The plausibility of Two Kingdoms Theology will thus erode with every degree our condition of secularity departs from our manifestly Christian moorings. In other words, it will likely be gone tomorrow. For today, then, I offer these critiques.

CULTURAL AMNESIA

W hy should I vaccinate my child for Polio? I suspect that is not the question you were expecting, but humor me for a moment. Why should I vaccinate my child for Polio? It seems such a needless thing. After all, there isn't anybody around who has Polio!

So forms part of the reasoning of a significant subculture in our society today, those who oppose giving children vaccinations. Why would we need to do that? After all, many, if not most, of the diseases we are inoculating our children against simply don't exist anymore. They don't pose much of a danger, so much so that the dangers of vaccination itself seem to outweigh the dangers of contracting the diseases.

At first glance it seems reasonable enough, until one points out that the reason nobody has Polio is that, well, we've been *vaccinating our children*. This is a common logical fallacy called "begging the question." The answer seems satisfactory until we see that the very thing being rejected (vaccination) actually provides the very basis for rejecting it! A "plausibility structure" is a sociological term that refers to a network of beliefs that make a given idea plausible. In this case, the plausibility structure for the anti-vaccination crusade, (i.e., the widespread lack of disease) is actually provided by the great success story of modern vaccinations themselves.

I could multiply instances of this kind of question-begging, but I wish to highlight just one: what makes *Pietism* possible? What has to be true for Pietism to thrive? What provides the foundation, or plausibility structure, of Pietism? There is no need to keep you in suspense: it is only widespread Christian cultural transformation that makes the rejection of Christian cultural transformation plausible.

The word "pietism" is one that I do not like. It is too easily confused with the perfectly good word "piety," one's reverence for and personal devotion to God. Piet*ism*, in the popular use of the term I am adopting here (originally it probably did not deserve pejorative scorn), is what happens when one comes to believe that the only thing of importance is one's personal devotion to God. It is better expressed by the word "Privatism."

Privatism is the belief that Christian truth has relevance for some segment of life smaller than all of life. It may be relevant, actually, for a lot of things: your private affairs; your personal devotional life; the way or manner in which you conduct yourself; how you relate to your spouse and family; how you conduct yourself in the church, and so forth. But nevertheless, there remain realms of life to which the truth claims of Christianity remain alien. Privatism is the belief that the Christian message is restricted in some way, usually restricted from having relevance or influence on public matters, or matters which concern believers and unbelievers alike as they co-exist in the world.

This is important for a simple reason: just as nature abhors a vacuum, so does culture. If Christians, embracing Privatism, cease to believe they have something unique to offer humanity in its cultural affairs, then cultural norms and customs will inevitably be provided by some other ideology. History is replete with examples of what those cultural norms are likely to be, and the prospects are not at all pleasant.

Unfortunately, it so happens that in our day we are experiencing something of a renaissance of Privatism. Certain theologians, not from segments of evangelicalism one would expect, are positively urging that Christians see their saving faith as not relevant to the public square or "common" matters involving Christians and non-Christians. This recent version of Privatism is, we should readily admit, an improvement on some other forms. Whereas older Privatists (represented in Anabaptist groups like the Amish or Mennonites) do not participate in the broader life of culture because they believe such things to be positively evil (and so they don't vote, serve on juries, or serve in the military), this version wants to affirm that cultural pursuits are, in fact, good. But they are only a lesser good on our hierarchy of priorities.

I am referring to the recent revival of a "Two Kingdoms" model for relating Christianity and culture, two preeminent representatives of which are Drs. Michael Horton and David VanDrunen of Westminster Seminary in California. I believe that the plausibility structure necessary for their arguments to work is provided by the fact that previous generations largely have not implemented their theological model. There is an initial persuasiveness or plausibility in the Two Kingdoms model that, on second glance, requires what I call *cultural amnesia*.

IT IS important first to provide a brief summary of Two Kingdoms teaching. I am not interested in knocking down straw-men, so let me give you a carefully considered and, I believe, accurate picture of the Two Kingdoms model.

The central dogma is that while God rules over and governs the entire world, he does so in two distinct ways. His rule is divided into two distinct realms, each with its own origin, its own norms, and its own destiny. The one realm has its origin in creation (recapitulated in the covenant with Noah) and is governed by God's general providence, its norms are provided by natural law or general revelation, and its destiny is strictly temporal— that is, it is destined to pass away. This realm they call the "common" or "civil" kingdom. It is made up of believers and unbelievers alike, and it encompasses all activities that are legitimately engaged in by everyone. This is the realm, in other words, common to all humanity. It includes things like civil government, marriage and family, the economic marketplace, arts, education, and, no doubt, much more.

The other realm, by way of contrast, has its origin in the new creation inaugurated by Christ and is governed by God's special grace in the gospel, its norms are provided by God's special revelation in the Bible, and its destiny is eternal. This realm they call the "special" or "redemptive" kingdom. It is made up strictly of believers, and it is found exclusively in the church of Jesus Christ. So, for example, only Christians take the Lord's Supper, but all sorts of people vote for public officials. Therefore, the Lord's Supper belongs to the "redemptive" kingdom and voting belongs to the "common" kingdom.

The crucial point is that while individual Christians actually inhabit both of these realms, the realms *themselves* do not overlap. This is the preeminent purpose of the Two Kingdoms paradigm: to avoid mixing or blurring these two realms. The origin of the one (creation) is distinct from the origin of the other (re-creation). The norms of the one (common, universal moral principles) are distinct from the norms of the other (special revelation, Scripture). The purpose or end of the one (temporal) is distinct from the purpose or end of the other (eternity). Living in these two kingdoms requires, accordingly, a dual ethic and a particular hierarchy of priorities.

When it comes to dealing with other believers, Christians experience a unity grounded in Christ, are bound to the norms of the gospel as revealed in Scripture, and together share in the hope of eternity. When dealing with unbelievers in the "common" realm, like, say, participating in PTA meetings or working on political campaigns or engaging in business negotiations, believers experience a unity with others grounded in creation (both parties are created in God's image), are bound to the common norms of natural law available to believer and unbeliever alike, and the parties together share in a modest this-worldly hope for a better life. As

VanDrunen explains in his book, *Living in God's Two King-doms* (Crossway, 2010, hereafter *LGTK*):

> A two-kingdoms doctrine distinguishes what is uniquely 'Christian' from what is simply 'human' [....] Generally speaking, to be 'human' here and now means living in the common kingdom under the Noahic covenant. Christians share the life and activities of the common kingdom with all human beings. What differentiates them from the rest of humanity is their identification with the redemptive kingdom and all that that entails.
>
> — LGTK, 167.

And so Christians should never confuse the two realms, what is merely "human" and what is uniquely "Christian." Particularly, since culture is a common kingdom phenomenon, it is illegitimate to speak of "redeeming" it. The language of grace, the vocabulary of the gospel, simply does not transfer or relate to the common order of creation. "Redeeming" or "transforming" culture is a category confusion, for it blatantly mixes the realms. Redemption only applies to the church, and cannot, by definition, apply to the common kingdom.

The cultural realm is governed by general providence and natural law, and, since God allegedly designed it that way, it gets along quite fine on those terms. Christians have no warrant to appeal to or apply God's special revelation to common cultural tasks, nor to seek to transform or redeem culture by the gospel. So VanDrunen writes:

We would do well, I believe, to discard familiar mantras about 'transformation' and especially 'redemption.' Nowhere does Scripture call us to such grandiose tasks. They are human dreams rather than God-given obligations.

— LGTK, 171.

Dissecting reality into Two Kingdoms is a huge project, as you might imagine, and there are myriad nuances and qualifications, as well as theological and ethical issues that, while I might wish, I simply cannot address here. One word of caution: very often in this debate people are given the impression that the "Two Kingdoms" question is the same thing as the "Church and State" question. That is, a Two Kingdoms advocate will sometimes suggest that if one does not embrace the model then one must believe in some kind of intolerant, theocratic government where freedom of religion and liberty of conscience are suppressed. This is a distraction, one easily contradicted by the perfectly respectable (and right) view that freedom of religion and liberty of conscience are themselves *Christian ideals*.

As we will see, Two Kingdoms Theology is not primarily about the separation of church from the state, though that might well be a related issue; it is, rather, about distinguishing the church from *everything else*—in VanDrunen's words, "what is uniquely 'Christian' from what is simply 'human.'"

With that overview, I wish now to focus on a single, recurring argument found in the works of David VanDrunen and, to a lesser extent, Michael Horton.

ALLOW me to present four lengthy quotations from VanDrunen's book, *Living in God's Two Kingdoms*. I do so, first, to demonstrate that this line of argument is pervasive. It is not an incidental, throw-away argument, as though the Two Kingdoms view could get along just fine without it. In fact, I have come to believe that this argument more than any other provides the plausibility of the Two Kingdoms model. Second, I want you to truly appreciate and feel the argument's tremendous rhetorical power.

> [T]hough education, work, and politics are distinct activities that require their own separate analysis, they all involve the life of the common kingdom under the Noahic covenant and require Christians, to some degree or another, to work alongside unbelievers in pursuing them. Learning, working, and voting are not uniquely Christian tasks, but common tasks. Christians should always be distinguished from unbelievers *subjectively*: they do all things by faith in Christ and for his glory. But as an *objective* matter, the standards of morality and excellence in the common kingdom are ordinarily the same for believers and unbelievers: they share these standards in common under God's authority in the covenant with Noah.
>
> — LGTK, 31.

Later, he returns to this theme:

[T]he normative standards for cultural activities are, in general, not *distinctively* Christian. By this I mean that the moral requirements that we expect of Christians in cultural work are ordinarily the same moral requirements that we expect of non-Christians, and the standards of excellence for such work are the same for believers and unbelievers. If you have ever asked someone who promotes 'Christian' cultural activity what that Christian activity should look like, that person has probably said something like the following: Christians should be honest, just, hardworking, environmentally responsible, and respectful to authority. Christians should certainly act in these ways, as many statements in the Bible indicate. But perhaps you have also stopped to consider whether these characteristics are uniquely Christian. If we hire a non-Christian plumber to work in our home or hire a non-Christian employee at our shop, for example, would we expect the same sort of behavior from them? Undoubtedly we would! These characteristics are not unique Christian obligations but are universal human obligations [....] Through the Noahic covenant God holds all people accountable for being honest, just, hardworking, environmentally responsible, and respectful to authority.

— LGTK, 168.

And again:

[T]he standards of excellence for cultural work are generally the same for believers and unbelievers. What constitutes excellence for the Christian engineer? Whether the bridge he designs holds up traffic. What constitutes excellence for the Christian plumber? Whether the pipes he fixes stop leaking [....] Activities such as building bridges and repairing broken pipes are general human activities, not uniquely Christian ones. Because God has upheld the natural order and sustained all human beings as his image-bearers through the Noahic covenant, these are activities of the common kingdom.

— LGTK, 169.

And finally, in his concluding chapter:

[A] writer promotes a 'contemporary Christian perspective on business,' which promotes the principles of fair trading practices for workers, healthy local businesses, and Christian-run start-up businesses that 'lovingly serve the needs of fellow citizens.' [These] principles are admirable, but there is nothing distinctively 'new creation' or 'Christian' about [...] them. All of these principles are grounded in the present created order and the terms of the Noahic covenant. The odds are good, in fact, that if you ask your unbelieving neighbor whether he believes in freedom, satisfaction of basic needs, ecological responsibility, fair trade, and healthy local businesses, he will heartily agree.

— LGTK, 193-4.

Michael Horton has likewise been in the habit of making this particular argument. In a number of writings, he derides the notion that there is a "Christian" way of, say, plumbing. But it goes even further: "[D]o we really need Christian pop music for our entertainment or Christian cookbooks? Is there really a Christian method of making stir-fry?" (*Where in the World is the Church?*, 196) It is, indeed, a humorous and very memorable way of making the argument.

IT IS POWERFUL. For the sake of discussion, I will call it the "Argument From Cultural Homogeneity." "Homogeneity" is just a fancy term meaning "sameness." There is a "sameness" about the norms and expectations for cultural pursuits among Christians and non-Christians. The normative standards and expectations for all sorts of cultural activities are the same irrespective of whether one is a Christian or not.

On its face, the fact is nearly self-attesting. Look around! Non-Christians do the same cultural tasks as Christians, from engineering to plumbing to voting to running businesses to making stir-fry, and all of it with the same norms and expectations! There is, in fact, a widespread homogenous understanding of cultural norms and expectations among believers and non-believers. So far, one can hardly disagree.

From this platform of cultural homogeneity, however, Horton and VanDrunen draw the conclusion that there is nothing distinctively Christian about cultural pursuits and that, therefore, efforts to "transform" culture are not only unbiblical, but superfluous. Why would we need to "transform" something on which everyone already agrees?

The argument can be broken down quite simply:

A. There is nothing distinctively "Christian" about cultural tasks because,

B. there is widespread cultural homogeneity.

C. This homogeneity is explained by, grounded in, or upheld by God's covenant with Noah.

It is this last item that first needs addressing. You may have noticed that in each and every quote from VanDrunen above, he included (C), a reference to God's covenant with Noah. Why? *Because without it the argument is no longer an argument.* What if I start with (B) and argue the other way around?

B. There is widespread cultural homogeneity because,

A. There is something distinctively "Christian" about cultural tasks, and Christians have been successful in promoting them.

This is precisely the conclusion VanDrunen does not want readers to draw. So it is not enough for him to simply point to the fact of cultural homogeneity. He has to *account* for it. What explains the fact that believers and unbelievers seem to have the same norms and expectations for cultural activities? In order to conclude that there are no distinctively "Christian" cultural norms, then cultural homogeneity must be grounded in something *other than Christian cultural norms*. Something else has to justify, explain, or underwrite the widespread agreement in cultural norms and expectations. In Two Kingdoms literature universally, without exception (an unusual uniformity in scholarly debates, and a happy one here), that "something else" is God's covenant with Noah.

And a lot of effort is expended in making the Noahic covenant the ground for cultural homogeneity. Indeed, an entire biblical theology is woven to support this claim. The problem is, to put it bluntly, that God's covenant with Noah cannot possibly be the ground for the cultural homogeneity we see around us.

Think about it for a moment. What is the covenant with Noah all about? At its core, it is about stability and regularity. Never again will God destroy all living creatures with a flood. God promises that "as long as the earth endures, seedtime and harvest, cold and heat, summer and winter, day and night will never cease" (Gen. 8:22). The refrain, "never again" is repeated three times (8:21; 9:11, 15). The sign of the rainbow will be an enduring sign of an "everlasting covenant" between God and all living creatures.

In other words, the commitments God makes in this covenant are inalterable. God's promises simply cannot fail. God commits to never destroy the earth by a flood? Sure enough, he has made good on this promise. God commits to uphold the regularity and uniformity of nature? Sure enough, God has made good on this promise. The sun still rises and winter still follows autumn. Now let us ask: what if God promised that there will be widespread homogeneity of cultural norms and expectations among the human race? Given God's nature and the nature of the Noahic covenant, then there has surely been, in fact, widespread cultural homogeneity *since the time of Noah*.

Few suggestions can be more empirically false. To

state the blindingly obvious: the history of the human race is not a history of cultural homogeneity. It is nothing but the record of cultures in conflict, most often resulting in warfare, bloodshed, persecution, and slavery. Very simply, if God's promises cannot fail and yet human history displays to us cultural conflict instead of homogeneity, we should entertain the notion that God never promised cultural homogeneity. And, in fact, he never did. There is nothing whatsoever in the Noahic covenant that promises such a thing.

And here we find a (perhaps sloppy or unintentional) sleight-of-hand in the argument. VanDrunen rightly points to the fact that God establishes a normative moral law against murder in this covenant. Objectively speaking, God promises three times that he will "demand an accounting" for the taking of human life. This does, obviously, establish an objective moral standard that continues in perpetuity.

But closer examination shows that VanDrunen does not appeal to the Noahic covenant primarily to validate an *objective* standard that God will maintain (who would dispute that?), but rather to explain why different peoples *subjectively* share the same norms and expectations. He appeals to Genesis 9, in other words, to explain why your *neighbor* shares your cultural standards. But Genesis 9 says nothing about whether your neighbor will understand God's moral law. It only establishes that *God* will stand by his moral law. VanDrunen uses a morally *prescriptive* text to prove, he imagines, a morally *descriptive* point. But the prescriptive text of Genesis 9 does not explain (much less describe) cross-cultural moral homogeneity.

Once the Noahic covenant fails as a rationale for current cultural homogeneity—i.e., the purpose for which it is invoked in the first place—all that is left is begging the question. There is no need for "Christian" cultural distinctives; look around! Everybody shares the same norms and expectations.

There is no need for the Polio vaccine; look around! *Nobody has Polio.*

THUS, the Two Kingdoms model for Christianity and culture begs the question. The fact that currently, in our present cultural location, there is widespread acknowledgment of norms and expectations regarding a wide array of cultural questions, (i.e., the reason why the "odds are good your neighbor will agree") needs a better explanation than terse, hand-waving references to the Noahic covenant. How did our cultural expectations get to be what they are? How and why is it that believers and non-believers alike have come to largely share the values of personal integrity, responsibility, commitment to the rule of law, general respect for human life, and so forth?

Our cultural homogeneity is notable not because it reveals a general principle traceable to the time of Noah, but because it is so patently the exception, not the rule, in human history. The answer is found precisely where Horton and VanDrunen dare not look: whatever measure of cultural homogeneity we see is the fruit of Christians promoting distinctively Christian cultural norms and expectations. I believe this is true with respect to any of their chosen metrics, whether it be engineering, plumbing, economic and business standards, moral and judicial principles, and, yes, as we will see, even the standards governing stir-fry.

TAKE THE ECONOMIC MARKETPLACE: One would think, given the rhetoric of the Two Kingdoms model, that unbelievers with no knowledge of or reference to God's special revelation or Christian distinctives naturally understand and accept the need for honesty, trustworthiness, justice, fair trade, good-faith dealing, just weights and measures, and the respect of private property. Yet the world is filled with places where corruption, deceit, bribery, theft, and economic stagnation are the norm, not the exception. It behooves us to ask: what places?

Peruvian economist Hernando De Soto tells us what places, and helpfully tells us in the subtitle of his book: *The Mystery of Capital: Why Capitalism Triumphs in the West and Fails Everywhere Else* (Basic Books, 2003). De Soto documents very carefully those regions of the world where economic productivity is stifled. Stifled, mind you, not by bad luck, lack of will power, or lack of resources. Stifled, rather, by government bureaucracies rife with corruption, graft, greed, an unwillingness to recognize and facilitate formal private property, and, of course, the host cultures that enable this dysfunction.

He and his researchers undertook a massive experiment to buy property or open businesses in the world's most economically challenged areas and found them to not share (or at least not to have implemented) certain western economic values. The findings were uniformly poor in Third World and former communist countries. Places which have what, exactly, in common? It is not De Soto's purpose to notice, but that need not deter us: these are places where Christianity has had the least cultural influence globally.

According to De Soto, capitalism's potential to bring economic prosperity only works in places where there is in place what he calls the "western legal property system." What an interesting phrase that is. There is a system of private property rights that brings incredible economic prosperity because of its basic principles of honesty, transparency, reliability, and accountability, but that system is strangely unique to that part of the world historically dominated by Christianity? That amazing fact is a doubtful coincidence.

Compare to VanDrunen's once-persuasive rhetorical appeal: "The odds are good, in fact, that if you ask your unbelieving neighbor whether he believes in freedom, satisfaction of basic needs, ecological responsibility, fair trade, and healthy local businesses, he will heartily agree" (p.194). No. Actually, outside of the western world, the odds are not nearly so good.

But surely everyone agrees that murder is wrong? That human life has intrinsic value, right? In individual liberty, correct? We cannot imagine that one need be influenced by Christian distinctives to believe those things. But believing there is cultural homogeneity on these issues is willful blindness.

Just in the last hundred years we have witnessed

gigantic cultural movements where the exact opposite is championed. We ought to remember that Mao Tse-Tung termed his deadly societal cleansing the "*Cultural* Revolution." Germans called their various 20th century quests for global hegemony a *Kulturkampf*, or "Culture struggle." These movements were driven, in other words, by *cultural* norms and expectations antithetical to anything Christians could affirm. Where were these shared, "common," homogenous values then? Where were they in the Rwanda of the 1990s or the Sudan of the 2000s?

"The odds are good," are they, that my neighbor will agree with me about the value of human life? My neighbor *where* and *when*? The answer is: your neighbor in the quiet, peaceful suburbs of the western world today.

Similarly with other moral issues: Why is there widespread denunciation of slavery in the world today? Because cultures uninfluenced by Christianity, with no contact with God's special revelation, reflecting merely on the created order decided to reverse millennia of slave-trading practice? Hardly. It took a persevering Christian culture-warrior named William Wilberforce to infuse western culture with its abhorrence of slavery.

BUT THOSE ARE MORAL ISSUES. What about the more objective disciplines such as science or engineering? Surely there is nothing distinctively Christian about looking under microscopes or building bridges, is there?

Many good, scholarly arguments have been made (and I will not rehearse them here) that the only good explanation for the explosion of science and technology in the western world is Christianity's doctrines of creation and providence. These doctrines produced a belief in the rationality (intelligibility) of the cosmos, as well as a linear view of history that makes the concept of progress possible. There is a reason science never flourished in the far East, in Asia, or in the Middle East. Science flourished where Christianity had the most influence. Again, a doubtful coincidence.

But what about those bridges and buildings? Surely there is widespread homogeneity about the normative standards governing engineering, right? Ask yourself: why is it that when massive earthquakes hit the United States of America, we speak of casualties (when and if there are any) in the single digits? Yet, in 1999, Turkey suffered an estimated 45,000 dead from a single earthquake. This happened in a highly industrialized part of the country where one would think good engineering would be a priority. An official Turkish investigation showed the death toll to be due primarily to poor engineering and construction. How can this be, if everyone agrees to the norms, standards, and ethics of engineering and construction?

Or how about the 2010 earthquake in Haiti, which leveled the entire country and left a staggering 300,000 people dead? Where were the homogenous, generally-understood principles of engineering then? Somehow (again, perhaps just coincidentally) the quality of the standards of engineering seem to greatly improve the closer you get to the peaceful suburbs of the modern western world. "The odds are good," are they, that my unbelieving neighbor shares my concern when it comes to building safety? Again, it behooves us to ask: my neighbor where and when?

BUT SURELY DR. HORTON has me on making stir-fry! There cannot possibly be a distinctively "Christian" way of preparing food, is there? I admit that it might sound silly. But it only sounds silly because Christian norms about food have *so permeated the western world that we simply no longer notice.* Think of it: can I prepare stir-fry for my Muslim neighbors with pork as the main protein? How about my Jewish neighbors? That would be what we would call a serious cultural *faux pas.* Maybe there is not so much cultural homogeneity about stir-fry, after all. What about my Hindu neighbors? Can I make beef stir-fry? Can I *flambé* the stir-fry with cooking sherry or brandy if I'm having my Buddhist neighbors over for dinner? The answer is no.

Horton's invocation of the sheer *freedom* involved in cooking, a fact so obvious it needs no explanation, actually betrays him. For there is essentially only one religious culture in the world that has no food regulations: Christianity. We rarely think of how profound that is. We take for granted that there is no "right way" to prepare food precisely because Jesus Christ declared all foods clean and his followers over the subsequent centuries culturally acted like it! The omnivores and foodies who both produce and watch the TV Food Network may not realize it, but their cultured taste is only celebrated because, by the influence of Christianity, in the western world *all foods are clean.* Outside of this consensus in western society (already crumbling, as the *halal* fast food restaurants cropping up in urban areas attest) food is not something about which there is widespread cultural homogeneity. So I beg to differ. In cultures uninfluenced by true *Christian* liberty, how you prepare your food can (quite literally) get you killed. Or just sued, in our thankfully more civilized context.

———

WHAT WE HAVE FOUND IS that arguably the most powerful rhetorical argument for the Privatism of the Two Kingdoms model fails completely. Making breezy and confident appeals to the Noahic covenant to explain why the "odds are good" that my neighbor might share my cultural norms and expectations simply will not do. The Argument From Cultural Homogeneity is an exercise in begging the question. It is no more compelling than being against the Polio vaccine because, after all, nobody has Polio.

What makes anti-vaccination movements possible? Forgetfulness. Amnesia. The blessing of a vaccine can be its curse. It enables its beneficiaries to take their health so for granted that we find them arguing against the very thing that preserves their health.

The blessing of Christian cultural influence can also be a curse. For it enables its beneficiaries to take its resulting cultural homogeneity so for granted that we find them arguing against the very thing that provides it. The only thing that makes this sort of Privatism possible, or even plausible, is cultural amnesia. People with amnesia forget how they got to where they are.

The hour is late. It is time for Christians in the west to remember, because if we forget how we attained all these relatively homogenous values we treasure (i.e., the cultural influence of Christianity), we will lose them altogether.

2

GRACE RESTORES & PERFECTS NATURE

My doctoral work focused on the theological anthropology of Herman Bavinck, the 19th century Dutch theologian, and culminated in a book not destined for a wide readership. But Bavinck's theological insights deserve wider recognition because they are just as relevant and practical today as they were when he wrote them a hundred years ago. Bavinck provided a theological blueprint for Christian cultural engagement. Its central insight is deceptively pithy and simple: "Grace restores and perfects nature."

HERMAN BAVINCK WAS BORN in 1854 and died in 1921, and in his lifetime and until recently he was primarily known as the right-hand man and closest colleague of Abraham Kuyper. Kuyper, a name you're more likely familiar with, was a giant of a man, figuratively (and, I suppose, one could argue literally). He was flamboyant, controversial, passionate, fiery, and incredibly accomplished. He was a journalist who founded a newspaper, a natural-born leader and organizer who led a successful political party, a churchman who successfully united two denominations, an educational visionary who founded the Free University of Amsterdam, a *bona fide* theologian in his own right, and—oh, yes—in his spare time served as Prime Minister of the Netherlands. Kuyper was at his best in the limelight. His right-hand man was, by way of contrast, quite the opposite. Herman Bavinck was not flamboyant. He was not fiery and passionate. He was quiet, measured, and level-headed. Next to Kuyper, it was perhaps inevitable that he would be something of the forgotten man in Dutch history.

After a hundred years, this is no longer true. Over the past decade his massive four-volume work of systematic theology has finally been translated into English from Dutch, and the wider world is now coming to realize the truth: it was Bavinck, even more than Kuyper, who was the theologian of their movement. Bavinck was every bit as brilliant a thinker as Kuyper, and every bit as accomplished.

A man of incredibly diverse interests, he not only wrote significant theological works, but also wrote about modern trends in philosophy, educational philosophy, modern science, and the (then) brand-new discipline of psychology. He was endlessly fascinated by the modern world, with its explosion of new technology, and he sought to evaluate cultural trends through the lenses of his Christian faith.

In addition to authoring one of the most significant, brilliant, and profound systematic theologies in many centuries, he succeeded Kuyper in the chair of systematics at the Free University of Amsterdam for twenty years, sat in the Dutch parliament, was admitted (a theologian, mind you!) to the Royal Academy of the Sciences, was knighted by the Queen of Holland, and was even hosted by President Teddy Roosevelt in the White House on his second trip to America in 1908. Bavinck, as you can see, was no wallflower. He was very much an accomplished man of the modern world.

It was not always this way. Bavinck was born the son of a minister and therefore, as often is the case, the son of a church community, with all the pressures and expectations that entails. His denomination was small, the kind where everybody knows everybody. It was somewhat doctrinally narrow, and tended toward Pietism (or what I've called "Privatism"). Their tendency was to be suspicious and to avoid the world. It is a story often told: the son of Pietist or fundamentalist parents, yearning to be free, breaks from the shackles of his youth and uncritically embraces all that he has been taught to avoid, right? Almost, but by God's grace not quite.

It could have turned out that way, but didn't. Bavinck attended his small denominational seminary in Kampen for one year before declaring to his parents and friends that he intended to go to school in Leiden. To give you the flavor, this is like someone attending Bob Jones University telling his fundamentalist-preacher father that he was enrolling next semester at the University of California at Berkeley! It was a shock to everyone, and viewed as betrayal by many. Bavinck knew he was going into the lion's den. He knew the theological liberalism then rampant in Leiden, but he wanted to hear it for himself. His fascination and curiosity compelled him.

Bavinck was indeed deeply challenged in Leiden, but by God's grace, and much prayer, he ultimately emerged with his faith intact. He did not emerge the *same,* mind you; he emerged as a mature man emerges from a great and serious spiritual struggle. It was a loss of innocence for him. He was saddened that in some ways aspects of his child-like faith had been lost; but for him there was no other way to truly know the enemies of the gospel and to truly know the challenges the church faced.

He knew that liberalism could never truly be faced if orthodox Christians never encountered any true liberals or never really sought to understand their point of view. The world could not be engaged if Christians refused to be a part of the world. In his post-Leiden years Bavinck found resolve, and over the next 40 years he became a champion of orthodox Christianity over against modern liberalism.

Here is why I rehearse this history: it is true he did not, in the end, embrace the siren-song of Leiden's liberalism. But neither was this, figuratively speaking, a *return to Kampen.* Bavinck refused the all-or-nothing choice posed by Privatism: either cultural isolation (equated with faithfulness) or cultural engagement (equated with worldliness). It was that very dualism, the chasm drawn between Christianity and culture, the church and the world, that became the intense, over-arching theological problem he devoted his entire life to resolving. Looking back, of course, his own biography might predict it. For Bavinck, it is not either Kampen or Leiden, faithfulness to God or engagement with the modern world. There simply must be a way of *faithfully* engaging the modern world. There must be, in other words, a way for the church not to fail culture by isolating itself from culture.

BAVINCK CAME to believe that the main reason Christians fail culture is that they don't have a *unified* world-and-life view. Instead, they tend to divide up the world into two realms that essentially have nothing to do with each other, or at least they exist side-by-side in a state of uncomfortable tension. There is the realm of "nature," the world God originally created, the world as it exists apart from his special grace revealed in Christ, the great wide world as we know it. The realm of nature consists of the rich cultural life of human civilization: civics, art, science, economics, and more. Then there is the realm of grace, the new creation in Christ, the bonds of Christian brotherhood in the church. This dichotomy in our day normally goes by the name of the "sacred/secular" distinction.

If you think about it, these two realms really just describe the two great works of God: creation "in the beginning" and re-creation "in Christ." Bavinck saw that most significant questions boil down to how we relate Christianity, God's re-creation of humanity in the image of Christ, to God's original creation. How does our identity in Christ (new creation) relate to the entire range of the rest of our lives, our work and vocation, our families and relationships, our civic responsibilities, arts, politics, all things that continually exist due to God's original creation? In other words, how does the truth of the gospel relate to the rest of life, Christianity to culture, grace to nature? It was this question more than any other that captivated Herman Bavinck. And he believed that most Christians sense this question in some measure. He wrote:

> At the bottom of every serious question lies the self-same problem: The relation of faith and knowledge, of theology and philosophy, of authority and reason, of head and heart, of Christianity and humanity, of religion and culture, of heavenly and earthly vocation, of religion and morality, of the contemplative and the active life, of Sabbath and workday, of church and state —all these and many other questions are determined by the problem of the relation between creation and re-creation, between the work of the Father and the work of the Son. Even the simple, common man finds himself caught up in this struggle whenever he senses the tension that exists between his earthly and heavenly calling.
>
> — "Common Grace," Calvin Theological Journal, 24 (1989): 55-56

Bavinck himself, not a simple, common man, devoted his life to helping the rest of us come to some resolution of this tension. And there I've just stated Herman Bavinck's first important observation: nature and grace need to relate to each other. They need "resolution." We must not view God's redemptive grace as being at war with God's original creation, or, as the Two Kingdoms model has it, his redemptive plans as something unrelated to his original purposes.

To allow Christianity and the church to stand unrelated to the rest of culture is to believe that the work of redemption is unrelated to the work of creation. In other words, if nature and grace exist side-by-side with unrelated purposes, then God's identity as Creator is unrelated to his identity as Redeemer. We ourselves, in turn, have an identity crisis. We will necessarily have a strong dichotomy between our "Christian" endeavors and "secular" ones. Once we start dividing the world into two realms, we end up dividing both God and ourselves, too.

THE ROOTS of this kind of dualism run deep, and they are found most obviously and influentially in Greek philosophy. Plato divided reality into "two," the realm of "ideals" and the material realm of our experience. Later, the Gnostics and Neoplatonists drew the distinction in terms of the "spiritual" realm and the "material" realm. In more recent history, philosopher Immanuel Kant made this division absolute: the "noumenal" realm is that of which we have no knowledge (the realm of "faith"), and the "phenomenal" realm is that of our empirical experience. And there are certainly other ways of conceiving it.

Here are two crucial points: first, in these views the two realms really *are* two realms, two states of existence. They are not figures of speech or different perspectives on one reality. This is to say, in philosophical terms, the dualism is *ontological*. Hang on to this because it will be important later.

Second, the line dividing these two realms always runs horizontally: there is always a "higher" realm, i.e., the important one, and a "lower" realm, i.e., the not-so-important one. Sometimes that is construed in even stronger terms: the "higher" realm is the good, and the "lower" realm is evil. Regardless of whether the "lower" realm is viewed as evil or in more benign terms, it is nevertheless always a realm of lesser importance and lesser value.

Christianity has not been immune from conceiving the world in these kinds of dualistic terms. There have always been groups of separatists who view the realm of nature, the "world," as evil, if to some extent a necessary evil. Anabaptists like the Amish or Mennonites would be examples. This is radical and frankly, a Gnostic view. We can summarize their view this way: Grace opposes nature, or, alternatively, Christianity opposes culture.

Others take a more benign view; the realm of nature is not evil, it is just incomplete. It is good as far as it goes, but what it really needs is supplementation from the realm of grace. This is the view of Roman Catholicism. The natural realm gets a passing grade, but if you consecrate it to the realm of grace (e.g., by way of baptism, holy water, signs of the cross), it really shines! Marriage may be a creation ordinance and ordinary people can naturally enjoy it; but to get the most out of it, it needs to be a *sacrament*. We can summarize Rome's view this way: Grace supplements or "elevates" nature, or, Christianity supplements or elevates culture.

Then there is another form of dualism: the Two Kingdoms model for relating Christianity and culture. This view is every bit as dualistic as the others, and in it the "higher" realm of redemption in Christ is the important one and the "lower" realm of culture is the less important one. In this view nature is neither evil nor incomplete. By God's common grace, it is good as far as it goes and needs no supplementation by grace.

Unfortunately, if this is maintained in an absolute way then nature is never influenced by grace because the two never meet. And the very purpose of the model—it must not be forgotten—is to keep the realms distinct. Whereas Rome wants grace to baptize and sacralize nature, The Two Kingdoms wants grace to mind its own business and remain in the four walls of the church where it belongs. I will summarize this way: grace occupies its own realm apart from nature, or, Christianity has nothing distinctive to offer culture. Nature and grace run on parallel tracks and it is unclear, at best, that they ever meet.

Herman Bavinck vigorously opposed all of these views, and it was not enough for him to rearrange things around the margins. Instead, he wanted to uproot dualism once and for all. Remember the two crucial things to remember about dualism? First, the two realms are "ontological." That is, they really *are* two realms, not two ways of speaking about one thing. Second, the line dividing the realms is always horizontal. There is always a "higher" and a "lower."

Herman Bavinck is about to help us eradicate dualism for us once and for all. I want you to mentally grasp that horizontal line in your hands.

Now crank it 90 degrees.

Now we have a vertical line. We no longer have two distinct, ontological realms. We have a timeline. We have two distinct *eras*. Two distinct periods in history. *We have a B.C. and an A.D., a "Before Christ" and a "Year of Our Lord."* The problem with dualism is that it always conceives of nature and grace, creation and re-creation, as two "storeys" on a building, one higher than the other, one that we should care about more than the other. Bavinck saw clearly that what we have are not storeys on a building, but a *story*, a history, a narrative.

Nature and grace are not two separate realms; they are instead, different states of affairs in the narrative plot of a story, what the Westminster Divines called the "estates" of man. The terms describe not two separate realms, but the same unified reality: the entire creation that God made "In the Beginning." Only now that one, unified reality of humanity, inclusive of its civilization and culture, are considered from two different ethical perspectives: they are either B.C. or A.D., "in Christ" or outside of him.

Christianity is not about two *realms*; it is about two *times*. And that is because history is, at its root, the story of the Father's good creation ruined by sin, restored by his Son, and perfected by his Holy Spirit. There are not two realms; there are two times, and the New Testament calls them "this age, and the age to come."

Jesus brought this "age to come" into the middle of history. The beginning of the coming age was always understood by the Jews to be the resurrection from the dead at the end of history. And now, in the middle of history, God has done the astonishing: he raised his Son from the dead as the firstfruits of the harvest. Paul can say with perfect accuracy that "if anyone is in Christ, he is a new creation: the old has gone, and the new has come" (2

Cor. 5:17)! Being in Christ means we are already participants in the new creation, the age to come.

Instead of two "storeys" on a building, then, nature and grace represent two ends of a narrative story. Nature is the "Once upon a time…," the creation as God originally made it. Grace is the "Happily ever after," the creation renewed by the work of Christ. Now you can begin to see why these things cannot be unrelated to each other. One thing we instinctively know about good stories is that the ending must really flow from the beginning.

The Greeks had a term they used for stories where the ending doesn't flow from the internal framework of the story: *deus ex machina*, the "god of the machine." In ancient Greek plays, sometimes the plot got too complicated, and to wrap things up they had a machine that would literally drop a god or goddess (Apollo, Athena, etc.) onto the stage who would arbitrarily just sort out the difficulties. This was not satisfying. We ourselves have Hollywood movies like this. The alien-invasion blockbuster film *Independence Day* built up the doom of humanity so effectively that by the time Jeff Goldblum's character has his drunken epiphany, "Let's give it a virus!" it seems utterly laughable by comparison (As is the fact that he ceases being intoxicated mere moments later. But I digress.) The point is that the second half barely, if at all, connects to the first.

Much better is the ending, a "Happily ever after," that flows organically from the "Once upon a time." In the best stories, the ending resolves something that was already a potential at the beginning. Cinderella, by all rights, should be master of her father's house upon his death, yet she sleeps in the fireplace. In her "happily ever after," she rules not just a house, but a kingdom. Job should be blessed by God for his faithfulness, yet has everything taken from him. His "happily ever after" finds him twice as prosperous as before. In both stories, the ending fulfills a potential outcome at the beginning.

So also the story of history. The perfection brought by Jesus Christ is a perfection God always intended for his creation. God's work of redemption after the fall was not a "Plan B." He did not change the plot or come up with something unrelated to his original purposes. He did not decide to junk his creation and move on to something else. The whole point of redemption is that God maintained his purposes for creation, so much so—he *"so loved the world"*—that he was willing to send his Son to die to make it happen. There is a reason Jesus Christ is described as the "Second Adam" and the "image of the invisible God." His work directly relates to and connects to God's original creation of Adam as the image of God.

If we conceive of nature and grace this way, then they are not unrelated, distinct and separate realms. For the terms describe the same reality: the world that God made. But they describe it at different "times" in the story: the world still wayward and far off, separated from God, or the world redeemed by God's grace in the Lord Jesus Christ.

Herman Bavinck's view can be summarized this way: "Grace restores and perfects nature." Note well: in this view grace does something to nature. Christ's work does something to God's wayward creation. The "age to come" has rather abruptly and unexpectedly intruded into "this age." The light shines in the darkness. Christianity actually does something to culture. It restores it from its sin and corruption and perfects it to its destiny, what it was always intended to be.

Now, some readers may be familiar with the literature produced by Two Kingdoms advocates and might think that I am wading into some tricky waters. Isn't it true that Dr. VanDrunen emphasizes the sort of "this age" and "age to come" biblical theology I'm suggesting? It is true. And yet he resolutely rejects the notion that grace restores and perfects nature. (Indeed, in one ill-conceived paper he suggested that this was Bavinck's concession to *modernism* rather than a recovery of the Reformation vision.) Either there is something Herman Bavinck is missing, or there is something VanDrunen is missing. I am confident it is the latter.

That is because he has not, in fact, escaped dualism. He has actually doubled-down on it. On the surface of things it appears that he has got rid of the old horizontal line of the two realms when he speaks of the timeline of "this age and the age to come." But his vertical line is, in fact, a horizontal line in disguise. Allow me to explain.

I have suggested that in an adequate biblical theology, the "Happily ever after" has to flow from the "Once upon a time." Grace has to organically relate to nature, re-creation to creation. VanDrunen, by contrast, believes that creation and re-creation represent two (almost) totally distinct realities. The world to come, the realm of the new creation, is a completely different realm than God's original creation. It is Plan B to the original Plan A or, to put it slightly differently, the single plan of God entailed that "Phase 2" represents a different reality than "Phase 1." We do not have one realm, God's creation, viewed in two different "times," under the wrath and curse, on the one hand, and liberated by Christ's grace on the other.

On the surface VanDrunen's view looks like a "story" rather than "storeys" on a building because he writes about it in terms of two ages, "this age" and "the age to come." But in fact ontological dualism (really, truly, two separate realms) makes its reentry into his theology right here. We are right back to a horizontal, not vertical line. The "new heavens and new earth" is an (almost) completely new heavens and a new earth, and the old and new (almost) never intersect.

I will address what I mean by that (almost) in a moment.

For the present, we can see this most clearly by looking at Romans Chapter 8. Paul tells us that

> the creation waits in eager expectation for the sons of God to be revealed. For the creation was subjected to frustration, not by its own choice, but by the will of the one who subjected it, in hope that the creation itself will be liberated from its bondage to decay and brought into the glorious freedom of the children of God.

> — ROMANS 8:19-21

Here Paul views God's original creation as positively longing for something. It is under bondage, and it groans for liberation and freedom. It longs, he tells us, for the resurrection. In other words, the resurrection of humanity will bring about the liberation of creation. Whatever else Paul is telling us, he is very clearly indicating that redemption has decisive consequences for the rest of creation.

Let us now examine VanDrunen's brief interaction with this text. After rehearsing Paul's argument that creation longs to be set free, he writes:

> To understand Paul's point, it is important to remember that *this present world was never meant to exist forever*. The first Adam was commissioned to finish his task in this world and then to rule in the world-to-come (Heb. 2:5). Thus when creation groans (Rom. 8:22) for something better, for 'the glory' that is coming (8:18), creation is not seeking an improvement of its present existence but the attainment of its original destiny. It longs to give way before the new heaven and new earth spoken of in 2 Peter 3 and Revelation 21.
>
> — LGTK, 65.

There are many things gravely wrong with this. Let me highlight a few.

First, he begins with a self-serving declaration, in italics: "To understand Paul's point, it is important to remember that *this present world was never meant to exist forever*." This is the scholarly equivalent of saying: "If you already agree with me, you will see that I am right." But the point he makes is crucial: he begins with the presupposition of dualism. Creation was never meant to last forever. Re-creation is a completely distinct reality.

Second, because he is committed to dualism, he inter-prets "freedom" and "liberation" to mean "giving way." Creation is groaning and longing not to be renewed, liberated from bondage and to experience freedom, but to "give way" or yield to the new creation. "Give way" is a novel, idiosyncratic, and untenable interpretation of Paul's "liberated into."

There is no way to sugar-coat this: VanDrunen appears to believe the creation longs for *euthanasia*: a "good death." On that day, on this view, "the mountains and hills will burst into song, and all the trees of the field will clap their hands" for... their impending *demise* (Is.55:12)? God's original creation is destined to completely pass away to make way for the new creation. And we can now see (if we haven't already) why the "Two Kingdoms" never mix. The "common" kingdom belongs to the old creation and the "redemptive" kingdom belongs to the new creation, and these two realities never mix.

I can scarcely imagine a worse interpretation of Paul's (or Isaiah's) point. His point is exactly what he says it is: creation longs to be liberated from its bondage to decay and to be brought into the glorious freedom of the chil-dren of God. It will experience this at the resurrection from the dead. The new creation is, therefore, the libera-tion and freedom of God's creation, not its demise. I suspect that VanDrunen front-loads his conclusion ("In order to understand Paul's point...") because he knows he is on dubious exegetical footing.

There is a danger, of course, of overemphasizing the continuity of the present world with the world to come and failing to recognize that the new creation also involves a radical transformation of present realities. But

VanDrunen is committed to the opposite error. He emphasizes *discontinuity* to the extent that the old and new are completely different realities altogether.

2 Peter 3 presents a substantially more cataclysmic vision of the end, and VanDrunen interprets its vision of cosmic burning, melting, and dissolving by fire as the complete dissolution of God's original creation. But these are *metallurgical* analogies: melting a substance by fire is a *purifying* act—it does not destroy the substance; it refines it. This is why Peter says that the result of this burning and dissolving is that "the earth and the works that are done on it will be *exposed*" (*hurethēsetai*, or "found out" 3:10). VanDrunen takes "exposed" to mean that all works are being destroyed. But on the metallurgical terms of the analogy "exposing works" means bringing them to light so that they may be judged, just as impurities in precious metals are "exposed" by the melting process and *may* then be removed (if the craftsman wishes). In Peter's vision, the final judgment is the radical separation of *sin* and its effects from God's creation; a separation that takes cataclysmic fire, to be sure, but not the annihilation of the substance of God's creation itself. This is nothing other than the Apostle Paul's understanding:

> If any man builds on this foundation using gold, silver, costly stones, wood, hay, or straw, his work will be shown for what it is, because the Day will bring it to light. It will be revealed with fire, and the fire will test the quality of each man's work.
>
> — 1 Corinthians 3:12-13

Moreover, Peter declares that the final judgment is according to the analogy of Noah's flood. But Noah's flood is not a picture of the kind of radical discontinuity VanDrunen imagines. After all, it involved an *ark*, a vessel designed precisely to preserve the "old" and bring it into the "new." VanDrunen insists that the Noah analogy means the wiping out of "all products of human culture" (p.68), but it amounts to a mere declaration, not an argument, and one I find incredibly dubious. At face value, it would mean the human race would enter the eschatological age not knowing how to start a fire, dig a well, manufacture a wheel, build a bridge, or play musical instruments. I think considerable skepticism is warranted.

VanDrunen's appeal to Revelation 18 fares no better. He notes that John's vision of "Babylon" is of a place "humming with cultural activity" (p.69). It is filled with kings, merchants, cargoes of precious metals, jewels, commodities of every kind, arts and music, craftsmen and industry. And, of course, all of it is utterly destroyed in an act of divine judgment. VanDrunen says "it is important to note that *Christians* presently participate in the cultural activities of Babylon" (p.69). Hence, we must draw the conclusion that the destruction of Babylon's cultural works equally spells the demise of the Christian's cultural works.

But here he has made a wholly illegitimate move. He casually equates the "Babylon" of Revelation with his idea of the *common kingdom* where Christians and non-Christians live out their lives in a common space. But in John's vision "Babylon" is presented as the absolute ethical *antithesis* of God's people.

Babylonians wear the mark of the beast, worship the beast, serve the beast, make war against the Lamb, and drink the blood of the saints. Babylon is not his "common kingdom" at all; it is the apex of evil, the kingdom of darkness in its ultimate worldly profile. God is not destroying her culture because culture is, in and of itself, somehow destined for destruction. He is destroying Babylon because her culture is *anti-Christ*: "Rejoice, saints and apostles and prophets! God has judged her *for the way she treated you*" (Rev. 18:20).

The Babylon of Revelation 18 is not, to understate matters, something in which Christians are participating; in fact, verse 4 explicitly warns against such participation. Moreover, the irony should not be missed that VanDrunen appeals to this text in an argument for the essential *neutrality* of culture (i.e., it need not and should not be specifically "Christian"); yet Babylon—culture and all—is here judged above all for its resistance to Jesus and enmity toward his people. A curious text for Two Kingdoms Theology to trumpet.

FINALLY—AND now returning to Romans 8—you may have noticed a few pages ago when I said that VanDrunen believes creation and re-creation are (almost) completely distinct realities. Given the overall thrust of his argument, you may be forgiven for wondering about that (almost). The truth is that he cannot possibly believe much of his own rhetoric. And, thankfully, he doesn't. For if the present creation completely passes away to make way for the new creation, then there cannot be, in the nature of the case, a *resurrection of the body*. There would be no point of continuity between this world and the next. There would be no hope, for it means that God is completely starting over.

VanDrunen admits that Paul goes on to speak of the resurrection, but he minimizes it as much as possible: "Our earthly bodies are the only part of the present world that Scripture says will be transformed and taken up into the world-to-come" (66). The *only* part. This, mind you, from a text emphasizing the groaning and longing of the "whole creation" for liberation (Rom. 8:22).

Here is what we have: dualism is driving VanDrunen headlong in the direction of denying the resurrection, precisely where dualism led the ancient Gnostics before him. Seeing the problem, as a Christian scholar he makes the necessary adjustment and allows for the resurrection of the body, but in a minimized way (i.e., "the *only* part"). The reality is that the corner into which he has painted himself requires something much more radical than tweaking and conceding the resurrection of the body, as if it were a minor point. Dualism has led his logic in precisely the opposite direction of the Apostle Paul's, and a mere acknowledgment of the resurrection will not suffice. He needs to abandon the dualism that leads his theology to this disastrous brink in the first place.

I suggest he start by following Bavinck's lead. He can grasp that horizontal line that separates this world and the age to come, that line that prevents them from inter-acting, that line that keeps heavenly realities from trans-forming any earthly realities (except our bodies, of course), and crank it 90 degrees. Now we have just one realm, one world, one creation that fell into sin, that is restored by the work of Jesus Christ, and perfected by the Holy Spirit. Now we have heavenly realities that transform earthly realities. And transforms not just bodies, but in the end answers the longing of the whole creation.

Herman Bavinck understood that dualism always mutes the gospel. It always puts something out of the gospel's reach. There is always something to which the gospel is alien. But Bavinck championed a full-orbed gospel: the good news that grace restores this corrupted world "far as the curse is found" and brings it to the perfection God always intended for it. The gospel is not content with just resurrected bodies; it wants souls, too, and minds, and hands and feet, and relationships. It wants the entire matrix of what it means to be human. And that means culture, too.

I conclude with some beautiful words by Herman Bavinck. It is my fervent hope that someday they will be a motto, a rallying cry for Christian cultural engagement every bit as memorable as Abraham Kuyper's famous "square inch."

[Christianity] creates no new cosmos but rather *makes the cosmos new*. It restores what was corrupted by sin. It atones the guilty and cures what is sick; the wounded it heals.

— Common Grace, 61.

3

A TWO KINGDOMS TEST

The increase of popularity of a "Two Kingdoms" model for understanding Christianity and culture continues unabated and there is, of course, much to consider. To do it full justice would require considering, among other things, its use of biblical theology, its view of the origin and purpose of common grace, and whether it avoids (as it dubiously claims) ontological dualism. But I have a narrow purpose in this essay. I wish to provide a simple test case to see whether a Two Kingdoms approach withstands biblical scrutiny.

In order to avoid distractions, it is important to remind ourselves exactly what it is we are discussing. At its heart the Two Kingdoms view insists on a strict distinction between two realms or "orders" over which God rules, one "common," and one "special." The former is governed by God's providential common grace and the latter by his special redemptive grace. The former is God's original creation and the latter is God's new creation. God's common grace kingdom consists of the natural life of humanity with its institutions: commerce and markets, law and politics, art and architecture and so forth—in a word, *culture*. God's special redemptive kingdom consists of God's specially redeemed people, the church—in a word, *cult*. The burden of a Two Kingdoms model is to avoid mixing or blurring these two realms. The origin of the one (creation) is distinct from the origin of the other (re-creation). The norms of the one (common, universal moral principles) are distinct from the norms of the other (special revelation, Scripture). The purpose or end of the one (temporal) is distinct from the purpose or end of the other (eschatological).

Part of the allure of a Two Kingdoms theory is precisely this neat, clean division. It claims in principle to enable Christians to properly order their priorities. Participating in common culture is worthy and commendable, but it should not be described as contributing to or building the kingdom of God. Political activism, art and entertainment, business and commerce must be kept in their places. They are good, but not belonging to the order of redemption. They are law-based, not grace-based. They are temporal, not eternal.

The paramount concern of the Two Kingdoms model is to deny that God's redemptive kingdom *transforms* temporal, common, non-redemptive cultural institutions. This, they believe, is the fatal conceit of Kuyper, Bavinck, and their Neo-Calvinist legacy. In the Two Kingdoms view the language of grace and the vocabulary of the gospel simply do not transfer or relate to the common order of creation. It is, they argue, a simple category confusion to speak of earthly, common institutions as being "redeemed," that is, belonging to the order ruled by God's special grace.

———

THIS CENTRAL CLAIM can be easily tested. There exists in the world an institution explicitly established by God in his original creation of humanity. Its *origin* is creation, not re-creation. This institution is enjoyed, in God's providence, by people of all colors, nationalities and creeds. It is not exclusive to Christians and, indeed, special grace is not strictly needed for it to be enjoyed by Muslims, Hindus, Buddhists, atheists or pagans. Thus, its *norms* are not explicitly Christian. Moreover, this institution is exclusively temporal and not eternal. Because it will not exist in the new heavens and the new earth, its *destiny* is decidedly not eschatological.

Given these characteristics, no better institution can be found to test the hypothesis of the Two Kingdoms model. If the theory is correct, then we will find in Scripture no expectation that this institution be "redeemed." We will find that God does not expect this institution to be governed by the ethics of special revelation, but rather by common and universal moral laws. We will find that this institution will not be spoken of using the language of the gospel, words like "grace" or "holiness." The institution of which I speak is, of course, marriage, or, more broadly, the family. And what we find in Scripture does not in any way conform to the theory of Two Kingdoms. Quite the contrary.

Given the realities of Jesus Christ's work of redemption, the very union between husbands and wives mysteriously becomes, with Genesis 2:24 as a proof text, a visible manifestation of "Christ and the church" (Eph. 5:32). Paul tells us the *ethical rationale* (norm) of a husband's actions toward his wife: "just as Christ loved the church" they are to love their wives (v.25). Paul tells us the *means* is special revelation: "by the washing with water through the word" (v.26). He tells us the *purpose*: "to make her *holy*" (v.26). Likewise, the ethical rationale of a wife's actions toward her husband is "as the church submits to Christ, so also wives should submit to their husbands in everything" (v.24).

This much is crystal clear: the gospel transforms the norms, the means, and the purpose of marriage. This transformation extends even beyond the husband/wife relationship. A child's relationship to his or her believing parents is rooted in the specially revealed 5th Commandment, and obedience is "in the Lord" (Eph. 6:1-3). Furthermore, Paul believes that the gospel so radically transforms this creational institution that the very faith of one member of the household renders the others in some sense *sanctified*:

> For the unbelieving husband has been sanctified through his wife, and the unbelieving wife has been sanctified through her believing husband. Otherwise your children would be unclean, but as it is, they are holy.
>
> — 1 Corinthians 7:14

At very least, what we find here is that the language of special grace and redemption—indeed, the gospel itself

—now thoroughly permeates what is indisputably a creational, common grace institution.

———————

LEST ONE THINK that I have built a straw-man, I should note that in *Living in God's Two Kingdoms*, VanDrunen stresses over and over again that the church is the *sole* institution and realm of redemptive grace (e.g., 102; 106; 114; 118; 120; 131; 133-34). To his credit, he notices the difficulty this creates for a concept of the "Christian family" (which should be a pure category confusion, on his terms), but he resolves the question with this opaque sentence:

> But though the New Testament does not create the family, it acknowledges its existence, confirms the authority structures within it, and speaks of *how Christ and the church make special use of the family in bestowing saving blessing.*
>
> — LGTK, 119.

Here we have the church "making *special* use" (a noteworthy adjective!) of a common institution in conferring "*saving* blessing." One wonders if VanDrunen has not entirely embraced Rome's view here: the redemptive sanctifies or "elevates" the common.

At any rate, the heretofore invincible boundaries between the Two Kingdoms now appear strangely permeable after all, even though this sentence appears in a section arguing for the family as a strictly "common" institution (119-120). On page 106 he says likewise, in a footnote, that the redemptive kingdom "makes special use" of the family, and promises further discussion. There is no further discussion, however, not even the slightest attempt to explain what the vague phrase "making special use" means. His entire discussion of the family concludes: "Though a common institution, the family is highly honored in the church" (120). Now we have "highly honored." One may be forgiven for finding this description inadequate to the overall task VanDrunen has assigned himself. Because it is.

We must conclude that the Two Kingdoms model fails the test, quite miserably. The New Testament unequivocally expects the gospel to transform an institution founded at creation, common to all humanity, and not destined for glory. This finding is far from incidental. It strikes at the very root of the model. But rather than going back to the drawing board, I believe its advocates should abandon it altogether for a theology that brings nature and grace into blessed harmony instead of stubborn division.

AFTERWORD

At first glance the voluminous catalogue of literature on Two Kingdoms Theology would seem to highlight the inadequacy of this small book. Admittedly, I have not, within this short compass, addressed all that ought to be addressed. There is the massive task of historical theology, for example, attempting to trace out what the Reformers and their heirs believed about these issues. There are many things besides to explore: Two Kingdoms Theology's view of the character, role, and purpose of common grace, whether and how it coheres with Augustine's "two cities," its rather narrowly institutional and ecclesial definition of the Kingdom of God, and whether it conceptually overlaps in any way with Kuyper's concept of "sphere sovereignty," for just a few examples.

But counting pages and themes can be deceiving.

In these three essays I have probed three aspects of Two Kingdoms Theology and found them wanting: its ubiquitous reliance on the question-begging Argument From Cultural Homogeneity, its latent and all-too-often explicit ontological dualism between nature and grace, and its utter failure to find its own view represented or endorsed in the pages of the New Testament on an inarguably perfect test case.

I count a failure of rhetoric, a failure of theology, and a failure of exegesis. Any one of those is enough for a theological system to require substantial alteration or rehabilitation. I leave it to the reader to decide what it means to have all three at once.

ABOUT THE AUTHOR

Brian G. Mattson serves as the Senior Scholar of Public Theology for the *Center For Cultural Leadership.*

He received a B.A. from Montana State University-Billings, an M.A.R. from Westminster Theological Seminary, and a Ph.D. in Systematic Theology from King's College, University of Aberdeen. He is author of a monograph on Herman Bavinck's theological anthropology, *Restored To Our Destiny* (Leiden: Brill, 2012)*; Politics & Evangelical Theology* (Createspace, 2012); a volume of collected essays, *The Bible As Bedtime Story* (SWB, 2018); as well as a short travelogue, *A Smith River Adventure* (Forthcoming: SWB, 2018).

He lives with his family in Billings, Montana.

www.drbrianmattson.com